STEPHEN BIESTY'S
INCREDIBLE
EXPLOSIONS

STEPHEN BIESTY'S
INCREDIBLE
EXPLOSIONS

ILLUSTRATED BY
STEPHEN BIESTY

WRITTEN BY
RICHARD PLATT

DORLING KINDERSLEY
LONDON • NEW YORK • STUTTGART

A DORLING KINDERSLEY BOOK

Art Editors Dorian Spencer Davies, Sharon Grant
Senior Art Editor C. David Gillingwater
Senior Editor John C. Miles
Production Louise Barratt

First published in 1996
by Dorling Kindersley Limited,
80 Strand, London WC2R 0RL

This Edition Published 2007

Illustrations copyright © 1996 Stephen Biesty
Compilation copyright © 1996 Dorling Kindersley Limited, London

A CIP catalogue record for this book is available
from the British Library

ISBN 978-0-7513-5442-3

GREETINGS EARTHLINGS!

The atomic drive and date controller on my space cruiser have broken down. Now, when I try to land on your planet I keep crashing at the wrong place and time. This is annoying for me, but it is a great way to meet Earthlings. You have all made me very welcome: artist Stephen Biesty helped me mend my craft when I crashed near his home. I told him of all the other places I had seen, and he drew them for me, so I had a souvenir of my trip to Earth. Perhaps you can spot my landing sites – there is one in each picture in this book.

Reproduced by Dot Gradations, Essex
Printed in Italy by L.E.G.O.

CONTENTS

TRACTION ENGINE

FIRE!

SPACE STATION

AIRPORT

TRACTION ENGINE

Hissing, steaming, clanking, and shaking the ground, traction engines are like mechanical dinosaurs. Almost extinct, they were once the most modern form of power. Traction engines first appeared around 1860. At first they drove stationary farm machinery such as threshers, that separated kernels of grain from their husks. Later engines pulled ploughs or heavy road wagons, and turned fairground rides. For a while, steam represented a bright, labour-saving future. But the reign of the traction engine was a short one. By the beginning of this century electric motors and internal combustion engines had begun to take over many of its tasks. Before long the puffing monsters were making their last journeys – to the scrap yard or museum.

On the belt
The engine could drive machinery, such as a threshing machine or a power saw, if a leather drive belt was looped around the flywheel. Often a traction engine would be used for threshing in autumn and winter, and as a power saw at other times of the year.

Forced water
Since the boiler is under steam pressure, water must be fed in forcibly with an injector. When the engine was running sweetly, the injector could often be heard "singing" quietly like a whistling kettle as it let jets of water into the boiler.

Steering
All traction engines were self-propelled, but early models required a horse for steering. Harnessed between the shafts of the engine, the nags did not have to work hard.

Creating steam
Heat to boil the steam comes from burning coal in the firebox. The stoker continually feeds the fire to keep up a good supply of hot gases. Hot gases from the firebox flow through tubes inside the boiler, making them so hot they boil the water, creating steam. The gases then flow from the boiler tubes into the smoke box. From here, waste heat and sparks are blown out through the chimney.

What the steam does
Steam from the boiler flows up around the cylinder into the valve chest. A sliding valve lets steam shoot through the valve chest into the cylinder, pushing the piston forwards. The valve then slides back to let steam in on the other side of the piston and push it backwards. As the piston slides backwards and forwards, it pulls on the connecting rod and forces the crankshaft around. The turning of the crankshaft drives the flywheel.

Spud pan and chain
Steering was never easy on a traction engine. It relied on a hefty chain attached to a large drum between the front wheels, called the spud pan. When the driver turned the steering wheel, the steering bar pulled on chains to turn the wheels.

Governor
The "governor" was a device which regulated the engine speed. It was a valve opened and closed by two spinning metal ball weights. When the weights spun too fast, centrifugal force moved them outwards, lifting the valve to let off steam and slow down the engine.

Water jacket
Too much heat could make the boiler blow up. So, apart from the open grate at the bottom, the firebox was entirely encased in a jacket of water.

Cylinder casing containing piston

Safety valve

Regulator chest

Whistle

Piston

Sliding valve

Connecting rod

Registration plate

Chimney barrel

Blower valve (blows steam up the chimney)

Exhaust pipe

Valve chest

Smoke box

Smoke box door lock

Smoke box door

Suspension springs

Water injector

Steel boiler

Steering chain

Boiler tubes heat water

Steering bar

Worm gear

Blasted boiler
Boiler explosions were a frequent cause of serious accidents. They usually happened when the driver interfered with the safety valve to increase speed. Among the best known was an 1880 explosion in the English town of Maidstone. The explosion killed the driver's mate, and blasted the whole neighbourhood with bits of the trailer and its load – sewage.

Engine driver
The traction engine drivers moved around from village to village, following the work. They had a reputation as dishonest, rowdy drunks. They earned 10 per cent more than the best-paid farm worker, and could afford to drink heavily.

The crew
Typically, a traction engine had a crew of three – steersman or driver, stoker, and oil boy. But sometimes extra men might be needed to run special machinery or look after a trailer.

No stopping
Traction engines were notoriously difficult to stop. Early engines had no brakes at all, and later ones had a barely effective handbrake which the driver operated with a wheel on the platform. Drivers slowed down on hills by shutting off steam and engaging reverse gear, but accidents were frequent.

Crunching gears
Most traction engines had at least one extra set of gear cogs for extra power for climbing hills – or extra control going downhill. But the driver usually had to stop altogether to slide a new gear into place. A really skilful driver could change gear on the move.

Tender behind
The area at the back where the driver sat, along with the water tank beneath and the coal hopper behind, was called the tender.

Topping up
A traction engine needed a lot of water, so a driver was always pleased to pass a stream of flowing water where he could top up the water tank below the tender.

Warm bedfellows
Driving often made traction engine crews so dirty that they could not find lodgings, so some drivers slept under their machines, warmed by the firebox.

Unsprung heroes
It took nerves of steel – and a great deal of natural padding – to survive the ordeal of a long journey on a steam roller or plough engine, for they had no springs whatsoever. Traction engines, fortunately, had a pair of hefty coil springs on the rear axle, though they were still far from comfortable.

Flywheel
Boiler pressure gauge
Handbrake wheel
Crankshaft
Gear change lever
Gears
Steering wheel
Driver's lunch of bread and dripping
Driver
Reversing lever
Toolbox
Coal bunker
Fire tools
Registration plate
Stoker
Water tank
Stoker's hole
Inlet to water injector
Hose for collecting water from roadside streams
Firebox
Open grate
Ash pan
Pieces of wood, called strakes, give wheels grip on bad roads

8NHP. WILLIAM ALLCHIN LᵀᴰD. 1907

FIRE!

BURNING IN A CITY BLOCK, FIRE IS LIKE A DANGEROUS MONSTER. It attacks your senses one by one. You can often smell the hot-tempered beast before you see it. As a fire grows by consuming everything in its path you hear its voice, first crackling then roaring in your ears. For town dwellers, the fire monster is an old enemy, and one that has never been far away. Today we're learning how to control the monster and curb its appetite. At home, simple safety precautions such as inexpensive smoke detectors warn of danger. If flames take hold, an emergency call brings brave fire fighters rushing to the blaze. Water from their hoses cools the flames, and creates steam that starves the fire of the air it needs to burn.

Aerial ladder

Don't panic
Recent research suggests that fire rarely causes panic. Though aware of the danger, people usually help each other escape. A stampede to safety happens only when victims believe the fire is about to cut off their escape route.

Anybody in?
Fire fighters must search every room to check that there's nobody unconscious, asleep, or perhaps too old or ill to move.

Fetching hoses
Lift shafts in new buildings are protected against fire, so fire fighters use them to rush hoses to floors where they are needed.

Bad buttons
Some lift buttons don't need pressing: the heat of your hand calls the lift. In a fire, they're fatal – the heat calls the lift to the burning floor.

Wet risers
In most nations, tall buildings must have wet risers – pipes that channel water to hydrants on each floor. Fire fighters connect hoses directly to the wet riser.

Hydraulic platform

Hydraulic snorkel

Chopper rescue
When the tallest buildings catch fire, rescue by helicopter may be the only escape for those trapped on the upper floors.

Alarming facts
Fire alarms should alert everyone in the building to the danger. Nevertheless, experience shows that when there are no other signs of fire, some people don't recognize the alarm signal, or they just prefer to ignore it.

In the dark
In a smoke-filled room, visibility is zero, and fire fighters have to navigate by touch alone. As they search, they pay out a cord, so that they can retrace their steps to safety.

Sprinklers at work
By spraying a fire with water, automatic sprinklers can put out flames before they take hold. Room temperatures much higher than 60°C (140°F) fracture a soft metal strip or a tiny glass bulb on the sprinkler nozzle; water then sprays out, covering about 12 sq m (130 sq ft).

Aerial platform rescues people

Smoke rises through ventilating shafts

Save my pianos!
Automatic sprinklers are not new. Henry S. Parmelee of Connecticut invented them in 1875 to protect his piano factory from fire. New England cotton mills made them a success – the fibres they processed made the mills a big fire risk, and without a sprinkler system, mill owners couldn't get fire insurance.

Fog nozzle sprays wide area

A long way down
The tallest turntable ladders reach floors up to 50 m (165 ft) above the ground.

Fireboat
When a dockside building bursts into flames, fire authorities can call on the city fireboat to help. It more often sprays water or foam on burning shipping.

Spreading smoke
A lift shaft can channel choking smoke everywhere. Newer buildings now incorporate pressurizing fans that force air into the lift shaft, keeping it free of smoke

Helicopter rescues victims

Sprinkler

Television news crew

Pumper vehicle

Low-flam fuel
Firetrucks run on diesel fuel, because it burns less easily than petrol, and is therefore less of a fire risk.

Hydrant

Hose supply
Fire fighters call the hose that takes water from the pump to the fire "delivery hose". Every appliance carries lengths of hose, but at really big fires a special hose-layer vehicle reels out long runs of hose exactly where they are needed.

Powerful pump

Stored lengths of hose

Tracking the fire
Inside the control centre, officers keep track of progress in controlling the fire.

Fire crew receives instructions

Getting dressed
On the way to the incident fire fighters climb into their heavy protective clothing.

Super pumper
The basic fire fighting appliance is a pumper – a huge pump on a truck chassis.

Fire control vehicle
Fire-fighters rely on up-to-date communications and computers to co-ordinate operations. At really big fires, the computer and communications centre itself goes on the road.

Snorkel
Hydraulic platforms, nicknamed "cherry-pickers" or "snorkels", lift fire fighters rapidly. However, in rescue operations they are not a complete replacement for long ladders, because the platform holds only four people.

Fire control van

Paramedics attend casualty on stretcher

Where's the fire exit?
People trying to escape from a burning building sometimes lose their lives because they look for an escape route that's familiar. To reach the doors and staircases they use daily they may walk right past fire exits.

Flaming floors
Most buildings have hollow areas under the floor, and often above suspended ceilings, too. Unless they are carefully partitioned off, these voids can spread the smoke from room to room.

SPACE STATION

WHICH WAY IS UP? HERE ON EARTH, THE ANSWER IS EASY. BUT TO AN ASTRONAUT on board a space station, it's a silly question. "Standing up" or "putting down a book" don't mean very much when everything is weightless. We get a sense of up and down from gravity. Scientists on the space station call this weightlessness "microgravity". They plan to use it to make ultra-pure crystals, or exotic alloys (mixtures) of metals. Microgravity can be a problem, though. Walking is hard when there's no gravity to press your feet against the "floor". Drinking is tough if the coffee floats around. American astronauts and Russian cosmonauts have found ways around these difficulties. The two nations hope to launch a joint space station soon. Plans have changed many times, but the joint craft may look roughly like this.

Satellite capture
One of the main uses of the space station is the repair of damaged satellites. The crew use the remote manipulator arm to capture the satellite, or to transfer it from the *Teleoperator* robot that collects the satellite from a distant orbit.

Remote manipulator arm

Teleoperator robot

Spaceplane
To travel between the space station and Earth, European crews use a spaceplane. Like the Space Shuttle, this rides into space on top of a rocket, and then flies back like a plane.

CREW AND SUPPLIES
SHUTTLE – USA

Cockpit controls

Bags of rubbish are collected to be carried back to Earth

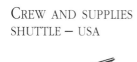

Forward reaction-control jets

Landing gear

Air purification
Lithium hydroxide cartridges purify the air in the cabins. Condensing the moisture from the astronauts' breath provides them with drinking water.

HEALTHCARE/HOSPITAL
MODULE – RUSSIA

Solar concentrators

Solar concentrators
Solar concentrators focus sunlight on water-filled tubes. The boiling water spins turbines that power generators.

Solar array

Radiators disperse heat from inside space station

Space junk
Solar arrays convert sunlight into valuable electricity. Their size makes them vulnerable to damage by orbiting debris left by earlier space missions. The station orbits at 8 km (5 miles) a second, and at this speed space junk just half the size of a pea does as much damage as a bowling ball travelling at 100 km (60 miles) an hour on Earth. There are more than 70,000 pieces of space junk this size in orbit.

Soyuz descent module

SCIENTIFIC
MODULE – RUSSIA

Remote manipulator arm
Astronauts can use the remote manipulator arm to move themselves towards objects away from the station.

Soyuz orbital module

Which way is up?
To give astronauts a sense of standing upright, each module has a "floor", two "walls", and a "ceiling". Lights are always in the ceiling, and frequently-needed supplies and controls are in the walls.

Docking manoeuvre
Cosmonauts are experts at docking manoeuvres: they have been using the technique to supply and re-crew their space stations since the 1960s. There are up to six ports where modules can dock.

Entering station at Russian end

Spektr satellite for geophysical studies

Docking port

Large airlock for EVA

Hatch

TV camera monitors exterior

Cosmonaut on EVA mission

MAINTENANCE
MODULE

Remote manipulator arm

LABORATORY MODULE

Formation flying
Not all experiments are housed in the pressurized parts. Some are attached to "free-flying" laboratories that orbit close to the station.

Free-flying laboratory

Eating a meal in weightless conditions

Exercise bicycle

Lavatory

Selecting a meal

HABITATION MODULE – USA

Spacewalk
Extravehicular activity (EVA or spacewalks) exposes crews to radiation. The station must be designed to minimize EVA time.

Rendezvous antenna

Space cinema
Space-station crews work hard, so a state-of-the-art entertainment system helps them to relax.

Airlock

Virtual reality cinema

Shower cabinet

OBSERVATION MODULE – USA

X-ray and ultra-violet telescopes

Camera

Astro-orientation equipment

Optical sight

Space telescopes
Onboard telescopes send astronomers very clear pictures of the sky. This is because the space station orbits above the atmosphere, which normally blurs pictures taken on Earth.

Space sickness

Tether

Water storage

Waste storage

Boom made of carbon fibre rods

Multispectral camera

CONNECTING MODULE – USA

Antenna for communicating with ground

Rope!
During space walks, astronauts used to sit in a costly jet-propelled armchair known as a Manned Manoeuvring Unit (MMU). This has now been replaced by a new high-tech solution: a length of rope!

Robot at work
Astronauts require food, water, oxygen, and sleep, all of which are scarce on the station. Robots need only electric power, of which there is plenty, to carry out routine maintenance functions.

Waste storage
Body waste and other space trash that is not re-used is stored for later transfer to a freighter. On re-entry to the earth's atmosphere, the craft and its contents simply burn up.

"Make mine a large one!"
Some recycled urine is used to replenish water supplies for cooking and drinking. *Bon appetit!*

EXPERIMENT MODULE – EUROPE

Scientist doing experiment using glove box

Dangerous work
Astronauts handling dangerous materials use a double-walled glove box to prevent contamination.

SPACE STATION

Pricey potatoes
The aim of space agriculture is to deliver nutrients and monitor growth automatically. Astronauts have grown the world's most expensive lettuce, soyabeans, and wheat, and a 160-kg (350-lb) crop of potatoes.

Experiment with germinating seeds in space

Exploded docking port

Crystal garden
One of the main aims of the space station is to grow protein crystals in microgravity (near weightless) conditions.

Space sickness
Even before the first space flights it was clear that some astronauts would suffer from motion sickness (their training aircraft was nicknamed the "Vomit Comet"). Scientists don't yet know why some crew suffer from space nausea, while others escape it.

Modular construction
An important feature of the space station is its modular construction. Each pressurized section is built of similar units, so that if one fails, a similar one can take its place.

AIRPORT

I F FLYING WAS AS CHAOTIC AS DRIVING, AIR TRAVEL would soon cease. The sky would be black with tiny aircraft. Mid-air collisions would be so common that newspapers wouldn't report them. At popular destinations planes would wait for the lights to change, revving their engines and hooting. Then they would race to see who was first down the runway. Of course, it wouldn't work. Flying is just too complex for each of us to own a plane. So at the airport we give up the privacy of our cars. We trust our luggage to a stranger and share the journey with others. Perhaps if we did the same on the roads our world would be a safer, more peaceful, and more pleasant place.

Air traffic control
The job of air traffic control is to route aircraft safely to their destination. To do this, controllers must make sure aircraft never come too close in flight, or when taking off and landing.

Keeping the skies safe
The approach control facility monitors aircraft beyond the circle handled by the visual control room.

Visual control

Lights out
Aircraft monitored by the approach control facility are tracked on radar screens. Older screens are dim, so staff work in a darkened room.

AIR TRAFFIC CONTROL

Nice view
Aircraft within 8 km (5 miles) of the airport are under the control of staff in the visual control room.

Approach control facility

Computer centre

A souvenir perhaps?
If you thought the business of airports was transport, you'd be wrong. Commercial operations, including gift shops, bars, and restaurants bring in up to 60 per cent of an airport's income.

TERMINAL 1ST FLOOR (DEPARTURES) GREEN FLOW

Bags of space
On average, every ten passengers on international flights have 13 pieces of checked luggage.

Search me
X-rays and searches stop would-be hijackers carrying on guns. However, there is no quick way to screen all checked bags for bombs.

Check in
International flights generally have computerized check-in. However, the procedure is simpler for domestic flights, and a manual system is quicker than a computer.

Multi-storey car park

Lift to car park levels

CAR PARK AND ROAD ACCESS

Underground access road

Counting cars
Airport car parks have to be vast. Los Angeles airport has nearly 19,000 spaces, and if all the cars left at once, they'd form a queue nearly 100 km (60 miles) long.

Distant gates
Big airports sprawl over huge areas, so "people movers" are needed for passengers transferring between flights. When Dallas-Fort Worth airport is complete, its most distant gates will be 7 km (4.5 miles) apart.

Underground railway train

Parking bill or phone number?
As anybody who has driven to an airport knows, the car park is a great money-spinner. It provides up to a sixth of the airport's profit.

Passenger check-in

Not so rapid access
Rapid transport systems linking national airports to the capital are popular with passengers: half of the passengers to London's Gatwick airport take the train.

Baggage reclaim carousel

Customs inspection area

Take the train
The belts carrying luggage are like a miniature railway complex within the terminal: Frankfurt airport has 40 km (25 miles) of track.

Automatic chaos
Computers help plan flights, but controllers still retain a manual system. If the computers break down, they write details of each flight on strips of cardboard, and shuffle them into a sequence of landing and take-off slots.

Runway
The tarmac strip on which aircraft land is called the runway. Its length depends on the type of aircraft using it and the altitude and climate of the airport.

Runway markings
Pilots use painted markings to judge their approach by day in good weather. A standard pattern of stripes marks the centre-line and boundaries, and helps pilots judge their altitude.

Green for go
A green bar marks the threshold – the start of the runway.

Approach lights
A standard pattern of lights visible only from the air points the way to the runway.

RUNWAY

Observation platform for public

Smoother than a baby's bottom
The runway surface is carefully maintained to keep it as smooth as a newly-laid road.

Runway may need to be 1.2 m (4 ft) thick to support the weight of the heaviest aircraft.

Gliding in
At night, coloured lights warn the pilot if the approach is too high or low.

Main radar

Noise annoys
Aircraft noise is intolerable for people living nearby. A recent study showed that they are twice as likely to kill themselves, and 60 per cent more likely to die in an accident. In addition, heart disease increased by 18 per cent.

Radar echo
The rotating dish of the main radar transmits a radio signal that bounces back from the aircraft. The reflections show up as blips on the air traffic controllers' screens.

APRON

Towing tractor
Powerful "tugs" pull the aircraft out on to the taxiway.

Apron
On the apron (paved area in front of the terminal) staff service the aircraft. They must work quickly because aircraft only make money when flying.

Power hungry
Aircraft engines generate electricity, but the supply stops when the engines do. A portable generator then supplies power.

Unloading baggage

Sorting it out
Luggage on the conveyor belt is usually hand sorted, but a few airports have an automatic system. This reads flight numbers from bar codes on tags. The system pushes the bags off the main belt into "branch lines" that lead to the right aircraft.

TERMINAL GROUND FLOOR (ARRIVALS) RED FLOW

Baggage on trolley

Crash tender

You're welcome!
The most welcoming airport is on the island of Curaçao. Two-thirds of the people visiting the airport go there to welcome friends or family, or to say "farewell". The least welcoming airport is Paris – only 7 per cent of visitors are greeters and senders.

Smelly rescue
Fire fighters are ready for everything. One major European airport is near a sewage treatment plant, and rescue teams are equipped with an inflatable boat and hovercraft, in case a plane overshoots the runway and lands in a sludge pond.

Fill 'er up!
Many airports have hydrants that pump aviation fuel from huge reservoirs. London's Heathrow airport has a store of 60 million litres (15.6 million gallons).

Fuel tanker

Ground crew services engine

Line of baggage
A typical 747 carries 800 pieces of checked baggage. Laid side-by-side, the suitcases would stretch six times the length of the aircraft.

Get a move on!
Baggage from an arriving 747 can be waiting on the carousels within 12 minutes, but some airlines take three times as long.

13

INDUSTRIAL REVOLUTION

Canals
Canals were the motorways of the early 19th century. A single horse could pull a heavy canal boat: on even on a good road, the same horse could move only 1/100th of the load.

Coal mine
Coal fuelled the industrial revolution. At some mines, pit-head winding gear winched tubs of coal from the seams deep underground. However, in most pits, children climbed ladders to carry the coal out of the mine.

Big burns
Overcrowding made large cities a terrible fire risk throughout history. Fires destroyed Dresden in 1491, London in 1666, and Copenhagen in 1728.

FIRE

London's burning!
A huge fire broke out in London in 1666, but it did not appear serious at first. When the fire started, the Lord Mayor of London dismissed the flames with the words "Pish, a woman might piss it out!" and went back to bed.

PLAGUE

"This is the end of the world..."
As large families crowded into small city houses, disease followed close behind. The biggest killer was bubonic plague – a disease spread by the fleas that lived on rats. An epidemic in the 14th century killed more than one quarter of Europe's population.

Let's get out of here!
Rich people fled when there was a plague. The poor had nowhere to go, and could not afford to travel, so they stayed – and died.

VIKINGS

Vikings
Viking peoples advanced from Scandinavia between 800 and 1100 AD, bringing with them traditions and skills.

Longboat
Skilled seamanship made Viking expansion possible. In their broad, open boats, the Vikings even crossed the Atlantic Ocean.

Factory

Railways
The first railway trains hauled coal, rather than passenger carriages.

Early locomotive

Flaming feathers
Diary-writer Samuel Pepys (1633-1703) watched the blaze, and felt sorry for the pigeons, saying they "hovered about the windows...till they burned their wings and fell down."

People fleeing fire

Fire fighting
17th-century fire fighters had little chance against a big blaze. They hauled water in tubs and pumped it onto the flames by hand.

Sealing a house
To prevent the spread of plague, city officials sealed the houses of victims, so that the affected family could not come out and infect others.

Plague pit

Plague pits
As more and more people died, the bodies were tipped into huge "plague pits" or mass graves.

Viking houses
Viking houses looked like upturned boats, and in ancient times they may even have been roofed with an old, leaky boat.

Viking house

Fire fighters

Coal mine

Canal

Demolishing houses to stop fire

Building a longboat

CITY CROSS-SECTION

TIME MACHINES REALLY DO EXIST. ARCHAEOLOGISTS – SCIENTISTS WHO study how our ancestors lived – use them to travel back into the past. They call their time machines "spades". With the aid of spades, trowels, and even soft brushes, archaeologists carefully remove layer upon layer of earth. Digging deeper and deeper, they travel back in time, for they know that, on any one spot, the objects close to the surface are more recent; those buried deepest are the oldest. As archaeologists sift through what remains of past people, they piece together pictures of vanished ages. Far below the city streets lies solid rock. Now palaeontologists take up the journey. They study fossils – stone casts of the animals and plants from the past. From fossils they can judge what life was like before humans arrived. The oldest rocks of all contain no fossils. Formed thousands of millions of years ago, before life began, they are a reminder that our Earth was once a ball of dust spinning in cold black space.

TODAY

Beneath the pavement
Underneath pedestrians' feet run the arteries of the city. Gas and water flow along pipes, and electric cables supply power. Sewers take waste away from buildings, and communications cables ferry data and telephone calls.

Dangerous digging
Workers on any city building site have to thread their way gingerly through the maze of underground pipes and cable, but they have another hazard to contend with: unexploded bombs.

Aerial bombing
World War II (1939-45) was the first war in which aerial bombardment played a major part. Bombs killed few citizens, but destroyed many houses: for each death in London, 35 people were made homeless.

WAR

Missed!
World War II bombs were "gravity bombs": They just fell to the ground when the bomber released them. Bombing was a hit-and-miss affair, and more than 90 per cent missed the target.

Factories
Europe's population grew rapidly in the 18th century, and towns grew especially fast. People moved to cities to find work as machine operators in the new factories.

High-rise buildings
Skyscrapers give the modern city a gap-toothed horizon. Two innovations made them possible. In 1854 American Elisha Otis (1811-1861) created the first safe lifts; they eliminated exhausting climbs for top-floor employees of even the highest building. Cheap steel-making was the other breakthrough. Instead of using thick walls to support upper storeys, a steel skeleton carried the weight.

Multi-storey car-park
Early multi-storey car-parks spared the motorist the helter-skelter experience of driving up and down winding ramps: instead a lift carried the vehicle to its space.

Winding ramp

Subway system
Because of traffic congestion, most major capital cities have created subway networks. London's Underground, built in 1863, is the oldest and the biggest, with 411 km (255 miles) of track underground and on the surface.

Traffic roundabout

Homeless people sheltering in cardboard boxes

Subway train in tunnel

Bomb damage

Bomb

Fire engine

Bomb crater

WINDMILL

Common sails
The simplest type of sails had a covering of canvas to catch the wind. To stop the sails turning dangerously fast in high winds, the miller reefed (tied back) part of the canvas to reduce the sail area.

Reefing names
Millers gave names to the different degrees of reefing. This sail is set to "sword point". Tying in more canvas set the sails to "dagger point". Spreading the canvas set them to "first reef".

Haul away!
The miller raised sacks of grain with winch powered by the sails. The mill boy tied on sacks at ground level, and jerked on the control rope to signal "haul away" to the miller above.

Wind-shaft
The sails rotated on the end of the huge wind-shaft. A small trapdoor above the wind-shaft allowed the miller to reach the sails for maintenance.

COMMON SAIL

Hem lath

Uplong

Canvas tied back to "sword point"

Curtain rail

Wind-shaft

Wind board

Sail stock

Shutter

SPRING SAIL

Miller filling grain bin

Brake

Brake wheel

Grain spout

Hopper

Frame called "horse" holds hopper

Mill-stone chest

Flour spout

PERCHED **ON A HIGH HILL-TOP** or towering over a flat plain, the unmistakable outline of an old windmill is visible for miles. The exposed position allowed the mill to catch the wind. A breeze spun the windmill's sails, and the miller used the wind power to grind grain into flour. Inside, a windmill is like a giant clock. Enormous gear wheels whirl all around, speeding up the turning action of the sails so that the rotation is fast enough for grinding. The similarity to a clock is no coincidence: in the 18th century, clocks and mills were the most complex mechanical devices in use. Today, factories grind flour, and only a few windmills survive, kept working to preserve a memory of bygone days.

Feed shoe

Drive shaft

Great spur-wheel

Stone-nut

Fantail

Meal bin

Post mill
To do their work, windmills had to face into the wind. The whole body of this mill rotates to face the wind, turning on a giant post that runs up the centre of the mill.

Freshly-ground meal bagged up and left to cool for several days

Brick roundhouse

Windmill origins
The windmill was probably invented in Persia (now Iran) in the seventh century, first appearing in Europe around 1180. According to some estimates, there were once 10,000 windmills in England alone.

Miller's thumb
To test the quality of flour, millers rubbed it between their thumbs and index fingers. This habit flattened their thumbs, making the hands of a miller instantly recognizable. Millers charged their customers by keeping some of the flour for themselves. Some grew wealthy by keeping more than their fair share.

Dangerous mills
Windmills were cramped, dangerous places and a careless miller could easily be crushed by the whirling wheels, each weighing as much as a small car. As well, millers with long hair risked catching it in the gears and being scalped.

Truck wheel moves to keep mill facing wind

Mill-boy ties chain to sacks to be hoisted to top floor

Sacks of grain to be milled

Path of the power
1. Wind pressure turns the sails.
2. The sails turn the wind-shaft.
3. The wind-shaft turns the huge brake wheel.
4. Cogs on the brake wheel drive round the smaller wallower.
5. A shaft from the wallower makes the great spur-wheel turn.
6. The great spur-wheel meshes with the two stone-nuts, turning them. 7. The stone-nuts turn the stones above.

Fantail

A small set of sails, called a fantail, kept the mill facing into the breeze. If the wind changed, it blew on the fantail, making it spin round. Gears transmitted the motion to the wheel below, driving the mill round until the fantail was again in the lee of the mill (out of the wind). Reduction gears ensured that even a light breeze on the fantail was sufficient to turn the great weight of the mill.

Wire machine

Wire brushes inside long drum of wooden hoops sieve out bran

Runner stone

Quarter-bar (leg)

Main-post supports mill

Scarf joint

Oak fillet

Solid brick pier

Structure

A massive vertical main-post provided support for the mill and sloping quarter-bars (legs) carried its weight to the ground. The horizontal cross-trees stopped the legs spreading, but the main post did not quite touch them.

Cross-tree

Wire machine

This powered sieve cleaned the bran (the grain's coarse, fibrous coating) and the wheatgerm from the flour. It required much less power than the mill-stones, so the miller operated it in light winds.

Brushes and flour

Meal entered the wire machine at the top, and revolving brushes forced it through the cylindrical sieve. Bran and germ could not pass through, and emerged at the cylinder's end.

Wallower

Foundation of roundhouse

SPRING SAIL EXPLODED

Shutter

Wind board

Hem lath

Iron thimble

Fulcrum pins

Sail spring

CLOTH SAIL EXPLODED

Sail stock

Wind board

Clamp

Sail bar

Uplong

Canvas sail cloth

Mill-stone

Tiled roof of roundhouse

Spring sails

Scottish miller and engineer Andrew Meikle (1719-1811) invented a radically improved spring sail in 1772. It had pivoting wooden shutters, like a Venetian blind, instead of canvas. Gusts of wind opened the shutters, spilling the wind harmlessly. Springs closed the shutters when the wind dropped.

Blowing a gale

Strong winds meant hard work for the miller. In a single gale the mill could grind more grain than in several months of ordinary winds.

Sails

The windmill's sweeps (sails) work like an aircraft propeller in reverse. The angle of the sail deflects the wind sideways, forcing the sail sideways – in the opposite direction.

Mill mice

Every mill had its mice, and it was not uncommon for the miller to find a mouse running around on the top of the spinning stones, trying to keep up with the rotation. There are ten mice visible in this mill – can you find them?

Putting on the brakes

The brake wheel turned within the brake: a wooden ring made in four sections. A heavy beam, the brake lever, held the brake tightly around the brake wheel, locking it in place with friction. To start the sails turning, the miller lifted the brake lever with a rope.

Path of the grain

1. The miller fills the grain-bin.
2. Grain falls down the grain spout into the hopper. 3. As the stone turns, a square piece of iron on its spindle shakes the shoe at the base of the hopper. 4. The shaking makes grain run from the hopper into the eye at the mill-stone's centre. 5. Meal (the milled grain) drops through a hole in the lower stone. 6. A chute channels the meal into a collecting hopper on the floor below.

EARLY SEAS

Teeming life
390 to 340 million years ago, during the Devonian period, teeming life in the warm seas began to evolve into the very first land animals.

First amphibians
Animals first struggled out of the water using their fins as primitive legs, gasping for breath with their inefficient lungs. Millions of years passed before they became fully adapted to life on land.

Simple molecules of life
Scientists can only speculate at how life began on Earth. However, the first living things on our planet were bacteria.

PRECAMBRIAN VOLCANOES

The cooling Earth
The Precambrian period stretches from the formation of the Earth to more than 570 million years ago. Over this period, the Earth's crust cooled, and the oldest rocks were forming.

Water
Seas and oceans formed from the water vapour pumped out by volcanoes. Pools of rainwater began to collect from about 3,800 million years ago.

BIG BANG

Big Bang
The universe may have begun as a single tiny particle with infinite mass. 10,000 million years ago it flew apart in a massive explosion, which we call the Big Bang.

Lungfish
Amphibia – the first land animals – probably evolved from three groups of Devonian lobe-finned fishes.

Trilobites
The closest living relations of these scampering sea creatures are crabs and lobsters. Most trilobites were smaller than an adult's hand, but a few grew to 75 cm (30 in) in length.

Cambrian oceans
530 million years ago, during the Cambrian period, there was no plant life on land. Even in the oceans, the only plants were slimy algae. Animal life was more advanced, however, and the water teemed with primitive worms and shellfish.

Atmosphere
The Earth's atmosphere was very thin until about 2,000 million years ago, when the first single-celled plants began to produce oxygen.

Volcanoes
Through cracks in the Earth's crust, huge amounts of molten rock burst out and flowed over the surrounding land. Volcanoes also produced large clouds of gas and water vapour.

Formation of the Earth
4,600 million years ago the Solar System began to form. Gas and dust condensed in space, drawn together by gravity. The heaviest particles massed in one spinning, eddying cloud of gas and matter, and gravitated towards each other to form the Earth.

Trilobite

Volcano

Molten rock

ROMANS

Conquerors
Spreading outwards from Italy, Roman warriors conquered almost all of southern and western Europe by 230 AD.

Fighting queen
The Roman rulers of eastern England whipped Celtic Queen Boudicca (?–62 AD) when her husband died. They then stole her land. Boudicca fought back by leading a rebellion in which her fighters slaughtered thousands of their hated Roman masters.

Orderly advance
Roman troops were highly disciplined fighters. When under attack, the troops could raise their long shields to make a continuous protective roof over their heads.

Roman soldiers

Pay-day tomorrow
Roman soldiers had a remarkably modern salary system. Stoppages from their pay even included a tombstone club, which paid for a funeral in instalments.

Megalith

Celtic warriors

EARLY PEOPLE

Emerging structures
The peoples of western Europe began to farm and domesticate animals 4–5,000 years ago – rather than gathering fruits and seeds, and hunting. This more settled way of life gave them time to develop social structures and religions.

Beaker people
About 4,000 BC communities of Beaker people spread across Europe. Archaeologists named them for the characteristic beaker pottery they made.

Megaliths
Neolithic people all over Europe built megaliths – upright stones, often arranged in circles and lines. Most scholars agree that they must have been used as part of religious celebrations.

Heavy haulage
Some of the most impressive stone circles in Europe are amazing feats of engineering. Their builders moved huge stones up to 320 km (200 miles).

Raising upright stones

Mammoth
The elephant-like woolly mammoth stalked Europe during the Pleistocene epoch, which began some 2.5 million years ago.

Stampeding mammoth

Flaying a mammoth

Pit-fall trap
Teams of hunters dug pits, concealing them with brushwood. Panicking the mammoths drove them across the pits and they fell in.

Vicious weapons
Ancient hunters may have used stone-tipped javelins to hunt mammoths.

DINOSAURS

Jurassic forest
Far beneath the streets of the modern city lie the remains of creatures that lived 150 million years ago. Most remarkable were the dinosaurs. Some were huge vegetarians that browsed on trees. Many dinosaurs, though, were ferocious meat-eaters.

Apatosaurus
This huge plant-eater weighed as much as four modern-day adult African elephants. It wandered the Jurassic forests of what is now the western United States.

Palm-like cycad

Allosaurus

Allosaurus
Though only a third of its size, Allosaurus made a meal of Apatosaurus. Palaeontologists are not sure, though, how Allosaurus fed. Some think that this dinosaur was a scavenger, feeding only on the remains of already-dead animals.

Trap

Apatosaurus

ANTARCTIC BASE

In THE MOST ISOLATED PLACE ON EARTH THE SUN NEVER SETS IN SUMMER — and winter is one long night. The climate is so hostile that no plant or animal can survive for long in the open. This place is the South Pole. It lies at the heart of Antarctica, a vast ice-covered continent. Antarctica was largely unexplored until seventy years ago. Today, scientists queue up to work at this cold and remote south polar base. Why? Because astronomers can peer at the stars for months on end, without daytime interrupting their work. Biologists gain a super-clean laboratory: Antarctic air is the purest on earth. And even the ice-cap itself is a remarkable archive. Locked in its layers of compressed snow is a 150,000-year-old record of the Earth's climate.

Polar night
Night begins in March with a twilight that lasts a month. "Morning" comes six months later. In the winter's sky, the stars circle continuously, without rising or setting as they do elsewhere on Earth.

Freewheeling
Tracked vehicles are the main form of transport at the pole. Coastal bases also use huge wheeled trucks called Deltas, plus motorcycles and snowmobiles.

Delta vehicle

Tracked vehicle

Weather station

Snowmobile

Steel arches form tunnel

Fuel storage

Garage entrance

Supplies storage

Cooking area

Roof arch rests on sides of ice trench

Dormitory area

Ancient meteorites (rocks from space) lodged in rock layers beneath ice

Explorer's memorial
This drawing is based on the Amundsen-Scott South Pole Station. Roald Amundsen (1872-1928) planted the Norwegian flag at the pole on 14 December 1911. The expedition led by British explorer Robert Scott (1869-1912) reached the pole a month later, but Scott's team perished on the return journey.

Underneath the arches
Steel arches provide much of the indoor space at the base. Their shape has been chosen so that the arches shed as much snow as possible.

The ozone hole
One of the most important jobs of the polar base is to monitor the Earth's ozone layer. Each year a hole in the ozone layer opens above Antarctica, and scientists at the base use their instruments to judge how much of a threat this poses.

Ice on the move
The ice sheet on which the polar station rests is moving slowly. The base moves along with it.

ICE MOVEMENT

Ice moves 10 m (33 ft) per year – the length of three small cars.

Don't throw water
The low temperatures at the base freeze all water vapour, drying wood buildings until they are like tinder. Fire is thus always a hazard.

Work in progress
Maintaining the base demands constant work. Many of the structures are nearing the end of their useful life, and the whole base will need replacing in a few years.

Polar day
...the poles, day and night don't take turns as they do on the rest of the planet. In "daytime" – which lasts the whole summer – the sun never sets: instead it just circles in the sky.

Airdrop
...supplies for the South Pole base are carried in by air. In summer aircraft can land on a prepared strip. Winter supplies are dropped by parachute.

Doomed dome
The most visible building at the base is the 50-m (165-ft) wide geodesic dome. However, the aluminium dome is gradually being covered by snow and ice, and this will eventually crush it.

Clear skies mean better views
Astronomers like using their telescopes at the pole because the sky is exceptionally clear. The biting frost freezes all the water vapour out of the atmosphere that normally blurs observations.

Eco-tourism
Sight-seeing flights do little harm to the fragile polar environment, but the impact of the 4,000 wealthy tourists who visit each year is controversial. Their 8,000 boots can damage coastal lichens that take decades to grow.

Supply drop

Geodesic dome

Radio mast

Weather
Meteorologists at the pole collect weather data for scientific research, and for guidance to aircraft flying over Antarctica.

Coastal bases
Most of the bases on Antarctica are on the coast, far from the South Pole itself.

Rocky research
Close to the coast, summer thaw exposes the rock surface. Parts of Antarctica are "dry valleys" which are never snow-covered. The dark colour of the exposed rock absorbs energy from the sun, warming the ground enough to evaporate any snow that falls.

Laboratory block

Danger: thick ice
An enormously thick sheet of ice covers Antarctica. Each layer of snow that falls on Antarctica compresses the snow below. The compressed snow, called firn, turns a bluish green colour. Ice cores taken by scientists provide a record of the Earth's climate over thousands of years.

Dome interior

This ice cream's cold!
Cooks at the base have to learn some odd skills. Stored in the dome, ice cream sets solid and must be thawed in a microwave oven before it's soft enough to eat.

Moving earth
Antarctica is almost earthquake-free, but there are more than 10 seismological (earthquake recording) stations on the ice-cap. They log quakes originating elsewhere.

Weather balloon launch site

The 300 club
The staff overwintering at the base make most of their own entertainment. Some join "The 300 Club" – a society which gets its name from the joining ceremony. Would-be members run from the sauna into the snow wearing only shoes, thus experiencing a temperature drop of 300 degrees Fahrenheit.

It's cold here!
Antarctica holds the record for the coldest weather anywhere on earth. In 1983 the temperature at the Russian *Vostok* base dropped to -89.2°C (-128.6°F). Mercury thermometers stop working at -40°C (-40°F), and even spirit thermometers can freeze, so meteorologists have to use special thermometers.

Windy too
The polar continent is also the world's windiest place. In some places wind speeds reach 320 km/h (200 mph), and rarely drop below 48 km/h (30 mph).

Movie studio

In the world of movies, nothing is quite what it seems. Buildings that seem to tower on screen are just tiny models. The giant squid dragging a ship beneath the waves is a latex puppet. A space station turns out to be a large sheet of canvas. Making these illusions look convincing requires the skills of a huge team of people, including set designers, background painters, and model-makers. These specialists craft the film in a studio complex. Teams may work for months on tiny details of a set – only to see it flash by on the screen in a few seconds.

Studio city
The sound stages, where filming takes place, are like huge sheds. They are carefully soundproofed, so that the sensitive microphones don't pick up the noise from traffic and aircraft outside. Though this drawing shows filming taking place on three sets all at once, normally only one of them would be in use at any time.

The backroom boys (and girls)
The sound stage is vast and obvious, but it's only a small fraction of the whole. Clustered round the cavernous set there's a maze of small workshops. Inside them an army of technicians and support staff toil. Without their support the production would sink.

Animatronics
Model-makers mould latex foam into elaborate monster masks and screen creatures, such as a small squid. Tiny motors hidden inside the rubber skin control movement of the limbs, and facial expressions.

Distant illusion
Carpenters build a quarter-scale replica of the Buddha statue. When it appears in the background it will look like the full-size statue four times farther away. Without such perspective tricks, the studio would need to be four times as big.

Roof structure

Lighting rigs on all sides of sound stage

Buddha model remains unfinished where camera will not see it

Camera crew

Huge boulder ready to roll down the set

Architecture of sound stage

Enormous, heavily-soundproofed door

Arm of huge Buddha taken inside for assembly on set

Making small model of Buddha in carpenter's workshop

Model of squid

Film vault

Processing film for editing

Editor working at editing table

Matching up soundtrack and film

Sound mixing on mixing console

Recording sound effects

Producing the final soundtrack

Mattress for stuntmen to land on

Fitting a costume in wardrobe

The cutting room
The process of cutting (editing) film has been largely unchanged by technology. Most editors still cut and join a cutting print (positive copy) of film shot in the camera. This will be used as a guide for cutting the negative from which the final prints are made.

Matching sound and picture
The editor's assistant synchronises the film and sound-track, which is recorded on magnetic tape with sprocket-holes, just like film. The assistant checks that the "clap" sound at the start of each scene lines up with the film frame showing the clapperboard closing.

Keep the noise down!
Much of the film's soundtrack is recorded after shooting is finished. For footsteps, actors walk around on simulated patches of "gravel path" or "autumn leaves". The final sound of the film may consist of thirty or forty tracks mixed together.

Big building

...ound stages can be vast. The biggest, ...Pinewood Studios in England, could ...old over 570 double-decker buses.

Dry ice inside rocket for blast-off effect

Huge rocket model for Sci-fi film

Speedy sprayguns
Painted backdrops are often used because they are so cheap and quick to produce. Two painters might take just a few days to conjure up a background the size of a tennis court.

Studio city
The biggest studios are vast complexes of buildings sprawling over an area as large as some towns. Universal City in California is the biggest. Covering 1.7 sq km (0.6 sq miles), the studio has its own fire brigade, zoo, stables, and police department.

That sinking feeling
Stuntmen replace regular actors for dangerous sequences. Stunts are filmed from a distance and later edited carefully. Stuntmen stood in for women stars in the past, but laws have made this illegal in the United States. The studio can employ a stuntman in drag only when all available stuntwomen have refused the part.

Wet weekend
To simulate rivers, lakes, and oceans, set-builders create vast water-filled tanks. The largest tank ever built filled a disused German airship hangar. Constructed in 1929, the 600-m (2,000-ft) long tank represented Russia's River Volga.

Rubber crustacean
Like the small squid in the model shop, this giant is a latex model. It's a kind of huge puppet, realistic only on the side that faces the cameras. This doesn't mean it's harmless: the rubber shark in *Jaws* (US 1975, producer William S. Gilmore Jnr) accidentally sank the ship carrying the cast and crew, sending the camera to the seabed.

Stirring up a storm
To simulate a hurricane, movie-makers fix an aircraft propeller to a powerful electric motor. Besides a convincing storm, the vast fan creates a lot of noise, and a realistic soundtrack must be added later.

Mock-up of rocket cockpit

Wave-making machine

Painted backdrop of stormy ocean sky

Ship set sits in huge tank of water

Sprinklers making rain

Large wind machine

Crew sit inside head of giant latex squid working tentacles

Ship rocks on springs to give ocean effect

Camera crew filming sequence on miniature set

Scenery storage

Light storage

Props storage

Director watching rushes in projection room

Wigmaker

Hairdresser

Heavy make-up (the devil)

Light make-up (stunning beauty)

Dressing room

Canteen

Publicity staff designing posters

Crew filming under water

Stills lab

"10,000 centurion's uniforms, please"
The wardrobe department supplies all the costumes. The audience sees major stars in close-up, so the costumes they wear must be authentic in every detail. Crowd scenes require vast numbers of costumes: on the 1951 movie, *Quo vadis,* the wardrobe department kept track of 29,000 outfits.

First look
Each studio has a tiny cinema, or projection room, of its own. There the director views the "rushes" – quick prints of all the scenes shot the previous day.

Camera crew
The camera operator has an assistant, who checks, cleans, and maintains the camera, and focuses the lens. The clapper-loader marks the start and end of each scene by clapping the clapperboard and is responsible for loading the film. The key grip on the movie is responsible for moving the camera.

VENICE

IMAGINE A CITY IN THE SEA. HALF SINKING, HALF FLOATING, ITS ROOFS AND GLITTERING towers rise mysteriously from swirling mist. This magic place was Venice in the 17th century. Already 11 centuries old, the city had begun as a mudbank refuge from wars on Italy's mainland. Protected from attack by its shallow lagoon, Venice grew into a great world power. An exclusive club of noblemen led by the Doge (duke) ruled Venice ruthlessly. They became wealthy by controlling overland trade between Asia and Europe. The discovery of a sea route to Asia ended the monopoly in 1488; and despite the centuries of decline that followed, the city's fabulous beauty and legendary art treasures survived almost unchanged. The picture below shows the central section of the city.

Doge
The Doge of Venice (left) wore elaborate robes made of costly fabrics. He also wore a pointed golden cap called the *cornu*.

Canals
Instead of streets, Venice is criss-crossed by water-filled canals. The biggest, the Grand Canal, is wide and lined with marble palaces. Others are tiny, and one even goes right underneath a church!

Piazza
St Mark's Piazza is a vast square, roughly the size of 45 tennis courts. It has always been the centre of life in the city.

Help!
"Streets full of water, please advise" cabled Robert Benchley (1889-1945) when he saw the city's thoroughfares. His telegram was a joke, but every visitor must share a little of the American writer's surprise on first glimpsing the Venetian canals.

Campanile
The famous Campanile (bell tower) of St Mark dominates the skyline. Completed in the 12th century, the tower has been restored several times. In the 15th century criminals dangled in iron cages from the south side as punishment.

Campanile bells
The five bells of the Campanile all had different meanings. The largest, *Marangona*, rang at the start and end of the day's work. *Nona* sounded at noon; and the smallest, *Maleficio*, signalled an execution.

Venetian symbol
The winged lion was St Mark's mascot. It appears on buildings all over Venice.

Granary
Large stocks of flour and grain in the warehouses (*Fontegheto della farina*) enabled the rulers of Venice to keep down bread prices and avoid food riots.

Mint
At the *Zecca*, (Mint), workers struck the gold ducats that were the currency of Venice. The coin kept its constant size and purity for more than 500 years, but eventually became known as the *zecchino*. From this word we get the word "sequin".

Books shelved
Venetians began planning a public library around 1360, but the building to house it was not completed until 1591.

Foundations
The buildings of Venice rest on piles: thousands of timber posts hammered into the clay of the lagoon bed.

Though Venice is less than 5 km (3 miles) long, the city's 177 canals total 45 km (28 miles).

Piles are made of Istrian pine: the wood gets harder as it ages.

Campanile

Rialto bridge

Grand Canal

Piazza

Granary

Merchant ship brings grain

Mint

Library

Layout of buildings with canals between

Bridges
Walking across all the bridges in Venice would be a huge task. There are so many that even guide books lose count. The famous Rialto bridge, which spans the Grand Canal, was designed by the architect Andrea Palladio (1508-1580).

Venice and visitors
Venice has always been a well-oiled tourist machine, finely tuned to separate visitors from their money as quickly as possible. Even in the 14th century, 500 years before the word "tourist" was first used, the city had inspectors to check travellers' hotels.

Lagoon
Venice sits in a lagoon which separates it from Italy's mainland. In many places the water is only waist deep, but dredged channels allow large ships to reach the shore and to travel out into the Adriatic Sea.

St Mark's Basilica
Once the private chapel of the Doge's palace, the Basilica is named for St Mark, one of Jesus Christ's 12 disciples (followers). The *Pala d'Oro* is the Basilica's greatest treasure. This great altar screen is crafted from gold and studded with precious stones. It took 500 years to complete.

St Mark's

Doge's palace
In the palace the Doge and his family lived in legendary luxury: the wife of the 24th Doge was said to have bathed in morning dew collected by her servants.

Pala d'Oro

Prison cell

Council chamber

Chamber of the Great Council
The meeting room for Venice's governing body of aristocrats was huge. It had to be, for the Great Council had more than 1,200 members by 1311.

Bridge of Sighs

Terrible ten
After an attempt to overthrow the Doge in the 14th century, Venetians appointed a council of ten noblemen to make quick decisions. They had great power, and organized a secret service that extended to every possible corner of the known world.

Doge's palace

Unholy trinity
The most feared men in Venice were the three Inquisitors chosen from the Council of Ten. They dealt with matters of state security, and could order the death of almost anyone.

Gondola

Smaller city barge

Doge stands on prow (front) of barge

Gondolas
The hired rowboats of Venice, called gondolas, are like water taxis.

Dull hull
Wealthy families once richly decorated their private gondolas, but from 1562 these glitzy boats were outlawed.

Piazzetta

Death in Venice
The Piazzetta in front of the Piazza was the site for the city's public executions. Between the two columns the executioner hanged wrong-doers, or cut their heads off. Bored with humdrum slaughter, he buried three traitors alive here in 1405, leaving only their legs visible.

Bucintoro

Bucintoro
The Doge's barge, *Bucintoro*, was the grandest ship in the Venetian fleet. Once a year, the Doge sailed out into the lagoon on it for a ceremony that symbolized the city's control of the ocean.

Bridge of Sighs
This famous bridge links the Doge's Palace to the office of the Inquisitor. The name comes from the mournful sound that prisoners made as they crossed the canal, for they knew they faced execution or torture.

TOWER BRIDGE

L ONDON'S LANDMARK BRIDGE LOOKS LIKE A TALLER TWIN OF THE
city's famous Tower nearby. Yet for all the pinnacles and parapets,
the castle-like masonry is only skin deep. Under its stone cladding
the bridge has a skeleton of steel. Built at the end of the 19th century
to relieve traffic congestion, Tower Bridge is a bascule bridge.
When a tall ship sails up London's River Thames, the two
bascules, or leaves that carry the roadway, lift to allow
the ship to pass underneath.

Original paintwork
Painters covered the metalwork of the bridge with three
coats of "bright chocolate" paint before opening day.

Royal opening
The bridge had a royal opening in 1894. Excited crowds gazed
as the bridge opened. But not everything went according to plan.
Amplified sound was still 20 years in the future, so the royal
opening speeches were completely inaudible more than
a few feet from the platform.

Chain links
The bridges that link the piers to the
banks on either side are suspension
bridges; so the supports for the
roadway are called "chains",
despite the fact that they
are really girders.

Heavy see-saw!
The word *bascule* means "see-saw"
in French. On Tower Bridge, lead
and steel weights counterbalance
the bascules. Each weighs
325 tonnes (320 tons) – as
much as 40 African elephants.

Weighty wind
Each bascule, or leaf, weighs
1,220 tonnes (1,200 tons) and is 30 m
(100 ft) long. On a still day, little force
is needed to lift the bridge. Yet the brid[ge]
can still open against the strongest
gale-force gusts, equivalent to lifting
each leaf with 150 cars parked on it.

Tower of strength
The original specification for th[e]
bridge required that it should b[e]
capable of being armed with g[uns.]

*Spiral staircase
access to roof
space*

*Lift
winding
gear*

Heraldic achievement (crest)

Bascule

*High level
walkway*

*Bascule locking
bolt*

*Gothic revival Scottish
baronial architecture*

Suspension chains

*Interior steel
framework*

*Anchor tie to north
approach road*

*North
approach
road*

*Gas
lamp*

*Lift carries 25
passengers to
high level
walkway*

Stairs to first floor

*Control
cabin*

*Night-time
signal light*

*Levers to
operate
bridge*

*Anchor
tie inside
concrete block*

*Entrance to
the Tower of
London*

*Archway
leading to
"Dead Man's Hole"*

Dead Man's Hole
An archway under the north approach
road gave access to "Dead Man's Hole"
– a temporary morgue for bodies fished
out of the river close to the bridge.

*Pier clad
in Cornish
granite*

*Gault brickwork
in cement*

*Machinery
chamber contains
two lifting engines*

Lead counterweight

*Passageway
to accumulator
chamber*

Plunger

*Pig iron
weights*

Bridgemaster's perks
The bridge employed 80 people, 14 on watch at any
one time, including a Superintendent Engineer and
a Bridgemaster, who had an official residence nearby.

Open wide
The bridge had to provide a very wide
opening so that vast square-rigged sailing ships
could pass through easily under wind power.

Built on mud
The bridge foundations stand not on bedrock, but on
clay. To prevent the bridge from sinking, it rests on huge
foundations. The engineers kept the weight down to less
than the pressure of someone standing on your toe.

Slate covering roof

Steel framework

Glass-reinforced plastic cross

Plastic fantastic
Cast in iron, the heraldic achievement (crest) of the City of London decorated the bridge until World War II, when it was taken down for safety reasons. Today's replica is made of glass-reinforced plastic.

External stone cladding exploded off

Steel girders under stone cladding

Octagonal pillar supports tower

Tug
For many years there was a tugboat on stand-by at the bridge. Most people thought it was to rescue suicides who jumped from the bridge. Actually it was to pull sailing ships through the bridge in case the wind dropped.

Slates

Suspension chain

Anchor tie

Chimney for boilers

One of six arches containing boilers and pumping engines

Accumulator house

Accumulator cylinder

BRIDGE CLOSED

BRIDGE OPEN

Lifting the bridge 1
1. Boilers, which used 20 tonnes (19.7 tons) of coal a week, supplied steam to hydraulic pumps. 2. Huge hydraulic pumps used the steam pressure to spin great flywheels. These in turn pressurized water in wide pipes that run all over the bridge. 3. Until it was needed to operate the bridge, the pressurized water was stored in one of six huge cylinders.

Lifting the bridge 2
Each cylinder lifted a piston loaded with a 100-tonne (98.4-ton) weight so that it rose 11 m (35 ft). 4. To lift the bridge, valves opened allowing the pressurized water to flow to hydraulic motors. These turned gear wheels that drove round racks on the quadrants fixed to the bascules, which then lifted.

"Doodlebug"
Wartime bombs never hit the bridge, but there were some near misses. In July 1944, a "Doodlebug" (German flying bomb) narrowly missed the bridge, but landed on the tugboat just as the crew were changing, killing two crews.

Belt and braces
All the hydraulic equipment on the bridge was duplicated. If anything failed, the bridge could still open and close.

CROSS-SECTION OF SOUTH APPROACH ROAD

Gas lamp

Stoking boiler

Hydraulic pipelines run to and from engine rooms

Operator's cabin

Hydraulic motor

Concrete block

Coal bunker

Head of anchor tie

Pumping engine

Water tank

Quadrant

Operator's cabin
The operator's cabin had to be positioned carefully so that the bridge operator could see both the river and the roadway clearly. Levers like those in an old-fashioned railway signal box operated the bridge.

Warming the pipes
Pressurized water moved the leaves of the bridge. If the water froze in the supply pipes the bridge would not open or shut. So, in winter, hot water flowing in a second set of pipes alongside kept the pressure pipes warm.

HUMAN BODY

A TRIP THROUGH THE HUMAN BODY WOULD BE LIKE SURFING THROUGH THE VAST network of subways and sewers beneath a city. From the pounding heart, you'd slow gradually as the wide tunnels grew narrower and lower, before cruising back to repeat the ride just a minute or so later. A trip around the lungs would be far quicker. Sucked down the ribbed trachea, you'd float along increasingly narrow tubes. Just a second later, hurricane-force winds would blow you out again. The brain controls the whole network, sending vital messages sparking through a web of tiny nerves.

Masticating muscle
The masseter muscle enables us to bite and is the body's strongest muscle. Normal bite pressure is about 75–100 kg (165–220 lb), but some people have a bite strength of nearly half a ton.

Reliable ticker
The human heart is an efficient and hard-wearing blood pump. It's only about the size of a fist, yet it can last for 70 years, pumping 30 times its own weight of blood a minute.

Not really bored
The yawn reflex draws air into the lungs when the brain needs more oxygen. This often happens after a long period of inactivity.

Claret of life
Our bodies contain about five litres (1.3 gallons) of blood – roughly half a bucketful. Three-fifths of it is coursing through our veins, while at any one moment our lungs contain about two and a half cups of blood. The rest is in the heart, arteries, and capillaries.

Lymphatic system
Another set of vessels in our body is the lymphatic system, which circulates a thin, milky liquid, called lymph. A line of defence and a source of nutrients, lymph contains disease-fighting white blood cells that combat infection. Filters in lymph vessels are known as glands, or nodes. When you are ill, germ-killing cells collect in the nodes to help you fight back.

Grey lump
Despite the awesome power of the brain, it's not much to look at. Some compare the brain's function with a computer's, but the human brain is many millions of times more powerful than even the biggest computers.

Hearing bones
Tiny bones in the ear amplify the vibrations of the eardrum to enable us to hear quiet sounds. The stapes, or stirrup bone, is the smallest in the human body. It weighs 2–4.3 g (0.07–0.15 oz), about the same as a sugar cube.

No bones about it
The "funny bone" is actually the ulnar nerve, positioned next to the humerus.

Dura mater (membrane on top of pia mater) absorbs shock

Inner ear

Ear canal

Outer ear

Skin

Eustachian tube

Cerebellum

CROSS-SECTIONED CERVICAL (NECK) VERTEBRAE

Deltoid muscle

Lymph vessels and nodes clustered under armpit

Triceps

Humerus

Left cerebral hemisphere

Pia mater (membrane covering brain)

Brain stem

Skull made up of 20 bones

Right cerebral hemisphere

Olfactory bulb (senses odours)

Olfactory nerves in nasal cavity

Pericranium

Lachrimal (tear) gland

Facial muscles

Skin and facial hair

Rib cage

Liver

Biceps

Right lung

Heart

Trachea (windpipe)

Pleural sac

Muscles of chest with veins and arteries covering rib cage

Muscles in palm of hand

Fickle fingers of fate
The bones in our hands are the most complex part of our skeletons. There are 27 bones in each hand, giving us unrivalled abilities.

CROSS-SECTION OF THIGH SHOWING MUSCLE GROUPS, ARTERIES, VEINS, AND NERVES

Hot muscles
In seven minutes spent playing an energetic sport the body's muscles give off enough heat to boil one litre (.22 gal) of water.

Achilles tendon

Tarsus (ankle)

Nerves
Muscle
Ulna
Radius
Lumbar vertebrae
Wrist ligament
Kidney
Tendons
Sacrum and coccyx
Femoral nerve
Pelvic girdle
Ball and socket hip joint

Thigh muscles

Femur (thigh bone)

Fibula
Tibia

Calf muscles

Cluster of lymph nodes around groin
Tendon of thigh muscle

CROSS-SECTION OF CALF SHOWING MUSCLE GROUPS, ARTERIES, VEINS, AND NERVES

Strong structure
The body's 206 bones are roughly as strong as the same weight of steel or aluminium. If they were made of concrete, four times as much material (by weight) would be required for the same strength.

Skin deep
Skin is a complex organ. On the area of skin covered by a small plaster there are some 163 hairs, 250 oil glands, 1,600 sweat glands, and 3,750 nerve receptors.

Fatty tissue with veins
Abdominal muscles
Greater omentum (fatty pad)
Front (apex) of bladder
Small intestine
Rectum
Anus
Colon
Stomach
Bladder
Penis
Testicle
Patella (kneecap)
Thick, hairy skin (on most of body)
Knee joint showing various ligaments within joint
Synovial sheath containing knee joint
Thin, hairless skin (found on hands and feet)
Tendons, ligaments, and muscles of foot
Vessels of foot
Hallux (big toe)

Digestive system
The alimentary canal (gut), which extends from the mouth to the anus, is about 9 m (30 ft) long. After eating, it takes about 24 hours for the food to travel through the entire system.

Liver
Tucked under the lungs to the right of the abdomen, the liver is the body's heaviest internal organ, weighing about 1.5 kg (3 lb). One of its many functions is to filter blood.

Stomach ache
Hydrochloric acid in the stomach is strong enough to dissolve metal. Sometimes it burns a hole in the stomach lining itself, causing an ulcer. A coating of mucus helps prevent the stomach from self-digesting, and the stomach lining renews itself every three days.

Hefty appetites
In the West, people eat an average of 40 tonnes (39.4 tons) of food in their lifetime – enough to fill a container lorry.

Nice iced
Fresh urine is completely sterile – people without water have avoided death by dehydration by drinking it. Eating beetroot can colour the urine red; a diet of asparagus colours it green.

Ticklish question
Medical science cannot yet satisfactorily explain why it is impossible to tickle yourself.

GRAND CANYON

EACH YEAR, NEARLY FIVE MILLION PEOPLE FLOCK TO THE south-western United States to see ... nothing! They marvel at a vast chunk of emptiness, 15 km (10 miles) wide and more than 1,500 m (one mile) deep. The Grand Canyon is thus famous for what's not there. Of course, tourists really come to see what the huge gap reveals: a candy-striped fantasy of layered rock. The raging Colorado River created this spectacular gash when it carved its way through the rocks of Arizona, taking ten million years to complete its work. Just as amazing as the layer cake geology is the climate and wildlife of the canyon. The base is a desert where rocks gets hot enough to fry eggs in the summer sun. Yet high above on the rim there are pine forests where mountain lions hunt deer in freezing winter snows.

Count 'em
One of the first white men to see the canyon wrote: "Ours has been the first, and will doubtless be the last, party of whites to visit this profitless locality." Now nearly five million tourists visit each year!

Cliffs and slopes
Hard rocks form vertical cliffs; softer rocks weather into steep slopes.

Empire State Building

Splat!
Anybody falling from the rim of the canyon would soon strike the sloping sides, but if they had a clear drop to the bottom, they'd have about 35 seconds to admire the view on the way down.

No snow
Snow often dusts the canyon's high North Rim, but it almost never falls to the foot of the canyon.

Crossing the canyon
Backpackers crossing the canyon usually start on the higher and more remote North Rim. The rim-to-rim record is less than four hours, but most take 2-4 days.

Hang glider

Exhausted
Some hikers can't complete the climb; the park rangers carry them to the top on mules. These "drag-outs" must pay their fare before getting into the saddle.

Ocean liner

Winding path leads to bottom

That's deep
The Grand Canyon is deep enough in places to stack four Empire State Buildings, one on top of the other. Its maximum width at the base is equivalent to five ocean liners lined up bow-to-stern.

Car park

Boreal zone
The highest point in the canyon is the North Rim, parts of which are more than 2,480 m (8,140 ft) above sea level. The aspen, fir, and spruce trees are adapted to shed the heavy snows that fall each year.

Underground drainage leads down into canyon

Transition zone
Along the rim in parts of the canyon is the Transition zone. Its climate and wildlife resemble those of both the Boreal zone above and the Upper Sonoran zone below.

Piñon pine

Upper Sonoran zone
The life zone of the upper side of the canyon is called the Upper Sonoran zone. At the top, juniper and piñon pine tree grow, giving way

Dead-end donkeys
Rule 14 in the 1922 Grand Canyon manual instructs that "All domestic and grazed animals that die in the park shall be buried immediately."

Rules favour mules
Park rules state that when mules and hikers pass, the quadrupeds pass closest to the canyon side. This can be unnerving for bipeds when the trail is only a little over a mule-belly wide.

Paths
The main paths have been widened by blasting out in places, but there are also many steep tracks worn by animals.

Saguaro cactus

Cacti and scrub

NATIVE
AMERICAN
GRANARY

The canyon's dry climate preserves centuries-old baskets of grain.

Canyon dwellers
Native American People explored the canyon perhaps 40 centuries before Europeans first saw it. From about 500 BC the Anasazi people lived here. They built room-like grain stores high above the river, often under rock overhangs.

Native American granary

RIVER BANK

Lush riverbank

Lush riverbanks
In contrast to the desert landscape surrounding it, the riverbank is lush and green.

Damn that dam!
Far more water once flowed down the Colorado, but today Glen Canyon Dam regulates the river flow to generate electricity. When the folks of Phoenix, Las Vegas, and Tucson turn on their air conditioners, engineers at the dam open the sluices and "turn on" the Colorado.

Lower Sonoran zone
At the bottom of the canyon (and mostly at the western end), the Lower Sonoran zone is a desert environment. Scorpions, more deadly than rattlesnakes, scuttle between the cacti.

Map the gap
The Grand Canyon was one of the last places to be mapped in the USA. In 1869, Major John Wesley Powell and nine others travelled the river in boats, and the US Geological Survey produced basic maps in 1902. River maps appeared in 1923.

Burrowing creature

DESERT
LANDSCAPE

Layers of rock

It's hot down here
The wildlife at the foot of the canyon has adapted to the desert conditions. Many creatures stay in burrows by day, emerging only in the cool of the night.

Rough and smooth
The Colorado River drops about 600 m (2,000 ft) in the canyon: roughly 1.5 m each km (8 ft/mile). However, the descent is not even: some parts are gentle, but in other sections the river flows through ferocious rapids.

Down the river
Riding the river in a wooden rowing boat takes three weeks; the sport began in 1909, and commercial trips started in the 1930s. From the fifties, huge rafts with room for 30 began carrying passengers.

Waterfall

Helipad

Ancient wonder
The oldest rocks at the foot of the canyon formed 2,000 million years ago.

INDEX

ACKNOWLEDGMENTS

Dorling Kindersley would like to thank the
following people who helped in the
preparation of this book:

Lynn Bresler for the index
Constance Novis for editorial support
Bohdan Paraschak for research

B.A.A. plc, Heathrow
Jack Fryer and the Cranbrook Windmill
Association
Kent Fire Safety Division
Shelter, The National Campaign for
Homeless People
Shepperton Studios for access to sound
stages and workshops
Special thanks to:
Lt. Katherine A. McNitt, Station Chief,
National Oceanographic and Atmospheric
Administration,
Amundsen-Scott South Pole Station